MW00596417

Contents

INTRODUCTION

Success has a technical definition, a factual conceptualization and has different descriptions, but ideologically it means something different to every individual. What success means to your parent may be different than what it means to you and what it means to you may be different than what it means to your best friend. Through years of on-going empirical research regarding success and successful people, I have become very familiar with behaviors, themes, or what I like to call *ingredients* of success. From an encounter with Michael Jordan and playing side by side world renowned pianist Awadagin Pratt in my high school symphony, to the everyday successful blue collar worker in the community, I have discerned 10 themes (ingredients) to success. I have discovered that regardless of ethnicity, spiritual identification, sexual orientation, weight size, socioeconomic status, job, career field, purpose, etc., that these 10 ingredients continue to be the recipe for success. I cannot stress enough that "…certain…behaviors will clearly affect your ability be successful," (Frazier, 2008).

Throughout this book, I will use non-fictional short stories to bring each ingredient to life. No matter if it's your first time using these ingredients or if you're a master chef, you will find a psychological, emotional, spiritual, and psychical connection to these stories and you will better understand how to cook up an individualized recipe for your own success. In addition to the 10 ingredients, I've also included information that will open the access door to your success and also hold you accountable for the freedom you will experience as you *create* success.

I want you to grab your pen and notebook to take notes. I also want you to read this book on the center stage of your imagination. Are you ready?...Good...let's begin our travel to and through different areas of LIFE and the journey of SUCCESS.

Chapter 1

(Ingredient #1) – Talent Without Skill Means Nothing

In an interview with Charlie Rose, Will Smith talked about how talent without skill is futile...completely useless. "Unless you beat on your craft every day, your talent will never communicate to the world," he told Rose. Continuing to emphasize that without skill, your talent will fail you.

In my late teens and early twenties I traveled to numerous boxing gyms because I've always had a passion for hand to hand combat. As I traveled to different gyms, I noticed that there were usually two types of fighters. One group of fighters was kinesthetically gifted and the other was athletically degenerative. The kinesthetically gifted individuals had great reflexes, catlike movements, and natural ability. They could perform the types of moves in the ring that really couldn't be taught. You just had to have it...be born with it. The interesting thing about these fighters was that, they would rarely work hard. Most of them, male and female, seemed to believe that because they had natural ability, their talent alone would get them over and be enough to win fights without really training hard. The other group, the athletically degenerative type, couldn't throw a coordinated punch in slow motion. These fighters came in the gym with great heart but usually left with broken bones. Of the two groups of fighters, the latter worked like workhorses, arrived at the gym before the gym opened or the coaches arrived, begged the coaches to keep the doors open *just for another 30 minutes* after close, did the road work, the shadow boxing, ate healthy and did pretty much everything that the more gifted fighters refused to do. When an individual from each group of fighters met in the ring to spar or for the actual sanctioned fights, I usually saw the less gifted fighters annihilate the naturally gifted fighters. Don't get me wrong, the more talented fighters may have won the first round or two, but once round three, four, five –came, they didn't have any gas left and the less talented fighter, who had been working on their skill and building up endurance daily, took over. On quite a few occasions I even saw the wimpiest looking kids beating up and knocking out the so called tough guys in the community. Because of the lack of skill and training the gifted fighters put in, it was like Will Smith said, their talent failed them.

Chapter 2

(Ingredient #2) - Understand and Attack Your Fears

(Ingredient #3) -Trust Your Passion

In the interview with Rose, Smith also talked about how there was a time in his life where he was daunted by things; he was scared to do things because of his discomfort with an obstacle and the fear of failure. However, fear couldn't stop Will because he is a true stalwart. Will Smith said that he got to the point where he got sick and tired of being scared to do things, so he began attacking everything that he was scared to do. He didn't say exactly what these things were, but we can postulate that they were things he needed to conquer in order to become the person he is today. Some might say it may have been taking the chance to play a silly acting character in a play that may make him look whimsical. Others might say it was stepping in front of tens of thousands of fans to perform his rap songs. I never met Will Smith, so I can only assume what the things were. What I can say for certain is that he attacked his fears.

Fear keeps us from living our dreams. I like to tell others that *many people choose to not live their dreams, due to the fear of suffering through the NIGHTMARES. But it's these same people that are usually unaware that they're already living the nightmare and killing the DREAM.* Furthermore, I believe that there are more people living their dream than we think. How so? People have bad dreams. They wake up in horror and that is exactly what they are living in...horror!

In his book, *Make The Impossible Possible,* Chief Executive Officer of the Bidwell Manchester Craftsmen's Guild in Pittsburgh, Pennsylvania, Bill Strickland, provides one of, if not the greatest, weapons I've ever learned, to attack your fears. He recommends that you need to *trust your passion.* I had a quantum experience when I read this, to the point where I closed the book and started thinking about how this significantly applied to me and my past. For example, there was a point in my life in which I had a bad stuttering problem. I had difficulty expressing my thoughts because it was hard for me to communicate effectively. It was so bad that in school, I wouldn't raise my hand in class to answer questions, even if I knew the answer to the question –in fear that someone might laugh at me. I wouldn't even give class presentations to my peers because it was too intimidating of a task for me. As I started learning more about life coaching and life in general – which I believe is my purpose on earth- and increasing my awareness of other subjects, I got to the point where I started mixing ingredient #2 and #3. I was no longer subdued by my fears because I was more passionate about what I wanted to do than I was scared to do it.

Chapter 3

(Ingredient #4) – Preparation

There is a guy in Pittsburgh I know of who is a licensed clinical social worker, life coach, businessman, and also a good friend of mine. He told me stories about what it was like starting up his own business, trying to be a major player in the field of psychology and looking for the perfect opportunity to get in the game. I'll never forget the story he told me about the inception of his company which was a new entity in the field of psychotherapy. He was promoting his business everywhere that he went; Chicago, Atlanta, Rome, Puerto Rico, you name it. "One time I ran into [Recording Artist] Keyshia Cole when she had her reality show and was looking for a family therapist," he told me. What a great opportunity! He continued, "I told her all about my counseling background and my company. I saw her become interested in the things that I was saying. Then she asked me the question." When he said this, I got into the conversation as if I was really there. "What question?," I asked him. "She asked me where my office was located at. Shawn…I couldn't even continue the conversation with her." By now I'm ready to smack him in the face for losing out on the chance of a lifetime.

"Why couldn't you continue the conversation!?!," I aggressively asked him.

He finished the story with the unfortunate line, "Because I didn't even have an office yet."

The lesson here is that success will knock on your front door and present you with an opportunity, but if you are not prepared for it, it will pass you by.

Chapter 4

(Ingredient #5) – Surround Yourself with Good Influences and

Examples: People and Things

I'm not going to spend a multitude of time educating you about the importance of surrounding yourself with people who motivate, inspire, and bring out the best in you. However, I will say that if your desire is to become a great teacher but you're a sophomore in high school hanging around class clowns and people that are failing, I'm not sure how *successful* you will be in achieving your goal.

I do want to elaborate on how integral it is in your journey of success to surround yourself with positive "things." This is not talked about often when discerning "keys" to success. I know a man who is a retired military veteran and he lives in one of the lower socioeconomic areas of Pittsburgh. Lower socioeconomic...what a *nice* term. I know it as "the hood!" The interesting thing about this man is that as you approach his home, he has positive messages spray painted on the front and back doors. *Be the change you want to see, Life is what you make it, Yes you can!*. In the middle of the hood, this man's home sticks out like a sore thumb. He doesn't stop there though. As you walk into his home, he has magazine articles of people who inspire him, all over his walls. Warren Buffet, Gandhi, Nas, Jay-Z, Harriet Tubman, Wu Yajun, Tory Burch…the list goes on. Even when you go into his kitchen, he has paintings of fruits and vegetables with the saying *You are what you eat!* This man is surrounding himself with MENTAL PROJECTIONS, the things that he wants to EMBODY.

I know of another man, who I played high school and amateur athletics union (AAU) basketball with. His name was Justin. We called him "JM." JM was a very good point guard. For the majority of his high school career he was the best player in the entire city and one of the best in the state of Pennsylvania. JM would always tell us "I'm going to play in the NBA." I am not sure if anyone believed that he would actually play in the NBA but I'm sure he did. My favorite experience of JM is when he invited me over to his house one day to watch some TV and play basketball. I walked into his room and JM had every basketball magazine that you could think of laying on his floor.

It looked like his entire carpet was made out of basketball magazines. JM was what I call being ALL IN. He was serious about his vision and he too was surrounding himself with the things that he wanted to become.

So what does this mean for you? Well, if you want to be an architect, you need to get a ruler or a miniature compass for your key ring. If you want to be a photographer then you need to have pictures hanging up on your wall around your bedroom, have film in your car, and so on. These are the things that will be a daily, even hourly, reminder of what you need to do to achieve your vision.

Chapter 5

(Ingredient #6) – Hard Work and Dedication

The title of this chapter should be self explanatory; and I truly mean that. Hard work is harped upon so much that I think, over time, people have come to believe that it's a myth or fairy tale. But it's NOT. If you are not willing to make sacrifices and dedicate yourself to your craft, you WILL NOT get to where you want to get to. Am I coming off clear?…can you feel my seriousness and intensity? You've got to work hard and work *smart*. In an interview, Vivica Fox was asked about a new business venture that she was taking on at the time. The reporter inquired about if she was planning on working even harder. Vivica calmly said, "I don't necessarily want to work harder. I want to work smarter." She was not indicating that she wanted to cut corners or take the easy route. Her statement resonated with me because it provided me another quantum moment. I thought wow, Vivica is right. If you *make wise decisions*, you can be more *efficient* and efficacious in your modus operandi. For example, you can use a hammer and screw driver to put up drywall, but that would take a fairly long time to complete. It would be wiser and more efficient to use a power drill instead.

I loved watching interviews of boxer megastar Floyd Mayweather Jr. Journalists would excitingly ask him, "Floyd, aren't you worried that he's bigger, stronger, and more powerful than you!?!" Floyd would smile and reply, "You can be bigger than me, stronger than me…you could even be just as fast. But one thing you won't be is smarter than me inside of that ring." If you watch the 24/7 episode documentaries of the build up to his fights, Mayweather always screams *hard work!*, as his team screams back *dedication!* Floyd knows that these are two salient ingredients that got him to the highest level of this pugilistic sport. 50 cent commented that "You'll never really understand the significance of what Floyd Mayweather does until you see how he trains in the gym…This guy is unreal!" *Hard work!...Dedication!*

Chapter 6

(Ingredient #7) – Knowledge Is Power, But You Must Research

As Well

People always say knowledge is power but to me, that is a myth. KNOWLEDGE is NOT POWER. For the rest of your life, I want you to remember this, knowledge is *strength*; applied knowledge is power. When I trained as an amateur boxer, I was a heavy weight and I had a friend in the same weight class as me. His name is Aaron Scott. When we would lift weights he could never lift as much as me but his punch was always so much more powerful than mine and I couldn't understand why. I was stronger than him but he was more power than me and it frustrated me. I figured out how to fix this frustration by using a tip from the great Jim Rohn. Jim says, "Turn your frustrations to a fascination." This is exactly what I did; I began studying and figuring out how this was possible. I found out that in boxing, sometimes speed can equal power. The faster your punch gets to the target, the more powerful the impact can be. Aaron was not only more powerful than me, he was faster than me. He never really knew how powerful I was because…I couldn't hit him. I couldn't apply what I knew (**my knowledge**). But you can surely believe I knew how powerful he was because not only did he use his knowledge and strength, but he <u>applied it</u> by using his speed which made him <u>powerful</u>. It is the same with information. Not that it's a race, but the faster that you are able to gain the knowledge and actually apply it…the more powerful you will be.

Chapter 7

(Ingredient #8) – Creativity

You've got to be creative. If you are not creative, I recommend that you dig deep and learn how to be creative because it's a prominent ingredient in your own recipe for success. Bill Strickland said that in order to be successful, you've got to blaze your own trail.

When I began my personal development company PerspectVe LLC, I had no idea how to start a business. I just knew that I wanted to start a business. I began looking at other businesses similar to the one I wanted to start and specially focused on how they functioned. Once I recognized common themes (or *ingredients*) I began modeling them in my own creative way. Things that other businesses did that I didn't like, I simply did not do them or I changed it up and put my own flavor on it. I'm still doing this to this day...blazing my own trail. "Sometimes success comes simply because someone thinks that they can do it better," (Strickland, 2007). But you have got to be creative in how you go about it.

Chapter 8

(Ingredient #9) – Build Resilience

In an interview with radio host Angie Martinez, Jay-Z was asked what he thought about people calling him the illuminati. Jay responded by saying that people like him or President Barack Obama didn't get to where they have gotten by worrying about what people thought about them. More directly he said, "You've got to have thick skin."

Similarly, Strickland wrote about how, at the time of his book, he still lived four blocks from where he grew up at. There were low-income people who came to his center (The Manchester Bidwell Craftsmen's Guild) who didn't like the fact that Bill (an African American Man) wore suits or that some of his closest friends were rich and powerful white guys. He seemed to be pretty authentic in his response to how he felt about this. Bill said that "it stung"…it hurt. But he also said that it didn't affect him too much because as a leader he wasn't worried about fitting into someone else's preconceived mold. He's telling the reader that as *a leader*, you should not be worried about haters, critics, or any of that. There will be people who will try to bring you down. That is probably how they were brought up. This can be both friends and family. Here is something else that I tell people that I want you to interiorize: *don't always accept people telling you that you forgot where you came from, because the bigger picture is that many people have* **forgotten where they have wanted to go**.

Chapter 9

(Ingredient #10) – Want Success as Much as You Want to Breathe

You have got to *want success as much as you want to breathe*. I love that quote! There's a story that motivational speaker Eric Thomas tells about a young man who wanted to be successful. This young man met a successful guru. Shortly after the encounter, the guru gave the young man specific instructions to meet him at the beach at 4:00 am. Once they arrived at the beach, the next instruction from the guru was for the young man to walk out into the water until the water was about shoulder level. Shockingly, and against the young man's will, once he got to a spot where the water was a little above shoulder level, the guru grabbed his head and held it underneath the water. Instinctively, the young man started **fighting** to get back above water because he wanted **to breathe**. The ingredient here is that when you get to the point where you want to succeed as bad as you want to breathe, you will then be successful.

Chapter 10

Success Wants Something In Exchange

Co-creator of Facebook Mark Zuckerberg dropped out of college because of an alternative path available to chase his passion. Comedian Kevin Hart quit his job as a shoe salesman to pursue his passion for comedy. Recording artist Akon said that being an entertainer is anything but living "the easy life." He said that there was a point in his career when he was working so much that he did not see his own family for over eighteen months. What you must understand is that none of these men were as successful during their upbringing as they are today. Now, when these men work, they make significantly more during that specific time than what the average full time employee makes in an entire year.

The response I periodically get when I bring the stories of these men up still amazes me. People will say to me, "But come on Shawn...really!?! Mark Zuckerberg? Akon?...These people are THE BEST at what they do." I tell them, *you're damn right!* These men, along with many other men and women, work on their craft every day. If you work on your craft every day you will be in the top 2% of what you do.

Speaking of people in the top 2% of what they do, I recall reading that Michael Phelps worked out every day for four or five years straight; not taking a day off on his birthday or a holiday. Michael Jordan said that he would work out so hard in practice that by the time game night came; the game was easier than practice. This is the point where we should all aspire to be, the point where when the lights come on we are confident, excited, and ready to showcase our *talent* and *skills* (think ingredient #1) because we have been working on our craft more than others could imagine.

I understand that everyone is not into athletics and everyone is not going to be an entertainer. If your goal is to be a successful military officer, police woman, financial advisor, etc, you should still be making sacrifices and working towards being THE BEST. Think about something. When athletes and entertainers have problems in their own lives, they will fly around the world in order to find the best doctor, the best therapist, the best teachers, and so on. So if you work hard on your craft every day, you may find that one day the President of the United States needs your phone number because there is no one better to call for the job than YOU.

I believe that all of us want to be successful. But what most of us don't realize is that success is a *life form* of its own and IT WANTS SOMETHING in exchange. If success could talk, one of the only questions it would ask is "What are you going to give ME?" Anyone who has been successful in their life or achieved goals had to give up something. Be it their job, their time with their loved ones, their old ways of thinking, or their last dollar. They HAD to give up something. I found this out myself. I had a good paying job, excellent benefits, nice office, and I had some influence in the company. But this wasn't the type of success I wanted. When taking a look at what you want to do in life, you must understand that there are jobs, careers, and purposes. They are similar and sometimes used interchangeably, but they are not the same thing. In the bigger scheme of things they are all needed to provide all of the services that exist in the world. Here are the differences. If you have a job, you may get paid an hourly rate. If you have a career, you get paid a salary. But when you have a purpose, they can't pay you enough! Your purpose is going to be your passion. If you can find a way to put your passion into your job or your career, that would be great. However, employers rarely pay you what you're worth. My spiritual brother Darnell once told me (as he learned from a friend of his); in life you get paid what you negotiate. When I realized that I had outgrown the position I was in, I had some choices to make. I could have continued to collect a paycheck, knowing that I would still be miserable. But in doing that, I would have had to accept the fact that, for the rest of my life, I would only make the amount of money someone else thought I should make. That was not ok with me. I took the chance to invest in myself and I gave up my job, my benefits, and my salary. It has been one of the best decisions I have ever made in my life. I look at success like a barter system. If you really want to be successful, you are going to have to trade in something that you have in your possession; something that you cherish.

Chapter 11

Words of Wisdom

I've studied and continue to study several people from Nicki Minaj to Gandhi, Farrah Grey, Ellen DeGeneres, and 50 cent (even the original 50 cent who was a cold blooded killer). Legend says that the original 50 cent killed over 30 people. His motto was *I'm going to provide for me and my family by any means necessary...even if I've got to kill you.* I'm not encouraging any unhealthy, negative, or ominous behaviors, but he was successful at what he did. The point is that success has various forms, good and bad. It's just a matter of where you are putting your energy.

No matter how many people I continue to study, the common ingredients to their recipe for success are these 10 ingredients that we have been discussing throughout this book. I recommend that you get serious about figuring out how these 10 ingredients will apply to you in your own recipe for success. You must make this stuff apply to YOU.

There are several other ingredients for success but these are 10 integral ones. However, the ingredient that has not been added to the recipe, but is the most important one…is GOD. I'm not talking about simply praying either. You should not simply pray. I believe that *smart decisions bring prayer to fruition*. Your prayers need to be followed up by action and the more action you partake in, the more likely it is that your prayers will come into existence. All of the blessings that you have prayed or continue to pray for are already out there in the universe, but you have to go get them. I do not believe that God wants any lazy children so you better have the *I want it! I'm taking action!* attitude.

I am an extremely spiritual person and I love to read all of the deities because they all have profound information to offer. I also like where the Qur'an states "Rarely will God change the condition of a people, until THEY CHANGE what is within their souls." What that means is that if you won't change, nothing around you will change.

It has been an absolute pleasure sharing these moments of your life with you. I hope to become a reference point in your memory and I pray that this information becomes <u>applied</u> <u>knowledge</u> in your life. Read this book over and over again and make sure that all of your friends and family have copies for themselves so that you all can better your PerspectVe as a team and bring out the best in one another!

  You can reach me at www.PerspectVe.com. Remember to spell word PerspectVe without the "i", because to broaden your own horizons, sometimes you have to take yourself out of your own PerspectVe. Take care and I pray you a happy, healthy, and meaningful life of success through God.

References

Frazier, E. S. (2008). *MOST LIKELY TO SUCCEED: THE FRAZIER FORMULA FOR SUCCESSS (R).*

Florida: Infinite Possibilities Publishing Group, LLC.

Strickland, B. (2007). *Make the Impossible Possible.* New York: Doubleday.

RELAITONSHIP GEYED - This book tells the true story about a period in one man's life when he met a woman whose behavior and lifestyle inspired him to leave his life of inappropriate relationships with other women, partying, violence, and self-destruction. Continuing to reap the benefits of being happy and in-love years later, while hearing so many other people cry and anger about their relationship situation, the author was propelled to share 13 unique elements that influenced him to become a faithful one-woman-man in a fairy-tale-like relationship.

With each chapter readers will not only find themselves emotionally invested and entertained by the author's transparent style of writing, they will gain an increased ability to improve multiple areas of their relationship life.

Improved Thinking - There are people in life described as "old souls." They are young in age and they may be youthful in spirit, but their minds are filled with an awareness of information and knowledge far beyond their years. Their ability to listen, understand, reflect, and communicate certain depths of life, at such a young age, make them human anomalies. IMPROVED THINKING is a book series written by one of these human archetypes. This succession of books is filled with some of the most fascinating and unique accounts of human experiences, thoughts, ideas, philosophies, and quotes ever written; including an unveiling of captivating sports-ideologies that unite universal wisdom with physical movement and the athletic world.

In reading these texts line by line, page by page, the reader will experience a supreme connection of clarity and enlightenment that will gradually help them to achieve and maintain a state of being at peace with the world around them and the world within them. Whether you are a newcomer or an avid reader of this material, let us all enjoy this voyage of ideas…and the hope is that you get "IT"!…Improved Thinking that is.

Improved Thinking Volume II - There are people in life described as "old souls." They are young in age and they may be youthful in spirit, but their minds are filled with an awareness of information and knowledge far beyond their years. Their ability to listen, understand, reflect, and communicate certain depths of life, at such a young age, make them human anomalies. IMPROVED THINKING is a book series written by one of these human archetypes. This succession of books is filled with some of the most fascinating and unique accounts of human experiences, thoughts, ideas, philosophies, and quotes ever written; including an unveiling of captivating sports-ideologies that unite universal wisdom with physical movement and the athletic world.

In reading these texts line by line, page by page, the reader will experience a supreme connection of clarity and enlightenment that will gradually help them to achieve and maintain a state of being at peace with the world around them and the world within them. Whether you are a newcomer or an avid reader of this material, let us all enjoy this voyage of ideas...and the hope is that you get "IT"!...Improved Thinking that is.

IT

IMPROVED

THINKING

VOLUME III

BY SHAWN FRANCIS-COLEMAN, MS PC
PROFESSIONAL COUNSELOR
PERSPECTVE LLC

Improved Thinking Volume III – There are people in life
described as "old souls." They are young in age and they may
be youthful in spirit, but their minds are filled with an
awareness of information and knowledge far beyond their
years. Their ability to listen, understand, reflect, and
communicate certain depths of life, at such a young age,
make them human anomalies. IMPROVED THINKING is a
book series written by one of these human archetypes. This

succession of books is filled with some of the most fascinating and unique accounts of human experiences, thoughts, ideas, philosophies, and quotes ever written; including an unveiling of captivating sports-ideologies that unite universal wisdom with physical movement and the athletic world.

In reading these texts line by line, page by page, the reader will experience a supreme connection of clarity and enlightenment that will gradually help them to achieve and maintain a state of being at peace with the world around them and the world within them. Whether you are a newcomer or an avid reader of this material, let us all enjoy this voyage of ideas...and the hope is that you get "IT"!...Improved Thinking that is.

KILLING
Sexual
Violence

Effective Solutions That Have Been Ignored

SHAWN FRANCIS-COLEMAN, MS PC

Improved Thinking Volume III – Sexual violence and
sexual predatory behavior has perpetually been a traumatic
global issue. The human soul's physical, spiritual, emotional,
and mental bodies of countless people have been maliciously
attacked not only by other malevolent individuals and
groups but also by people who have suffered similar pain
themselves. This vicious cycle has turned some people into
monsters and has been considered to be normal in certain

places around the world to the point where some of the victims of these violent acts have learned to accept and tolerate it as a standard way of living.

Lives have been tragically disturbed, unspeakable images pervade the psyche of sufferers, and horrific grief accompanies people throughout their human existence...day after day, moment after moment, and into the lives of the next generations. But this can stop. This book has been solely created to help lethally inject the mind-state, attitudes, and other conditions that bread sexual violence. It provides effective solutions that have been overlooked and largely ignored. The strategies within this text fall outside of the traditional sexual violence awareness program material that has not addressed root causes of sexual violence. This literary orchestration utilizes each page to discuss integral components of killing sexual violence and sexual predatory behavior.

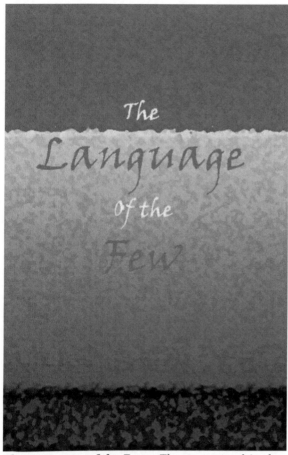

The Language of the Few – There are a multitude of languages spoken around the world. A single country may possess several different dialects; and on a continent – even more. There are individuals who are multilingual and fluent in various tongues but there are few people who are able to communicate with the universe symbolically. Over the course of time much of humanity has disregarded the most soulful form of communication; the language of symbolism.

The Language of the Few is one of Shawn Francis-Coleman's most influential and meaningful pieces of work to date. As a prominent psychotherapist, speaker, and student of life who recognizes the impact and power of trauma and problems within the lives of most people, Mr. Francis-Coleman helps each reader learn how to listen and communicate with the universe through situations, experiences, and life-events in a way that turns stress into strength and problems into power. Through learning and/or reconnecting with this forgotten language, readers will find an increased ability to use symbolism and spiritual alchemy to live a healthier, happier, more resilient, and fulfilling life.

Made in the USA
Middletown, DE
09 February 2022